LEADERS OF
ANCIENT GREECE

CLEISTHENES

Founder of
Athenian
Democracy

CLEISTHENES

Founder of Athenian Democracy

Sarah Parton

rosen
central

Published in 2004 by The Rosen Publishing Group, Inc.
29 East 21st Street, New York, NY 10010

Library of Congress Cataloging-in-Publication Data

Parton, Sarah.
Cleisthenes: founder of Athenian democracy / Sarah
Parton.
      p. cm. — (Leaders of ancient Greece)
Includes bibliographical references and index.
ISBN 0-8239-3826-3
1. Cleisthenes, of Athens, ca. 570–ca. 508 B.C.
2. Democracy—Greece—Athens—History—To 1500.
3. Athens (Greece)—Politics and government.
4. Statesmen—Greece—Athens—Biography.
I. Title. II. Series.
DF224.C54 P37 2003
938'.502'092—dc21

                                        2002007906

Manufactured in the United States of America

Cover image: The ruins of the Parthenon on the Acropolis,
the high hill at the center of the city of Athens. *Inset:* a
carving of an Athenian philosopher and his students.

CONTENTS

GREECE AT THE TIME OF CLEISTHENES

BLACK SEA

MACEDONIA

THRACE

● Sigeum

● Acanthus

AEGEAN SEA

● Phocaea

● Ephesus

● Chalcis

Delphi ● Thebes ● ● Eritrea

● Miletus

● Athens

● Corinth

PELOPONNESE

● Halicarnassus

Olympia ● Argos ●

● Sparta

IONIAN SEA

CRETE

MEDITERRANEAN SEA

THE HISTORICAL BACKGROUND

It is difficult to imagine our world without democracy—the "rule of the people." We assume that when we are adults we will be able to cast our votes in an election and choose a leader who will serve us. Most people think such a system is fair and just. It allows everyone who is eligible to express his or her opinion and to choose how he or she wishes to be ruled. It is difficult to think back to a time when there was no democracy anywhere.

In ancient Athens, in 508 BC, a leader called Cleisthenes reformed the way that his city was governed. The Athenians invented democracy, and Cleisthenes was the man who had the ideas to make it work. Although this system was not named "democracy" at the time, Cleisthenes realized that it was possible to govern a city effectively while still giving every

An artist's reconstruction of some typical Athenian houses

citizen a chance to have a voice in that government. It was Cleisthenes who the scholar Aristotle described as the "leader and champion of the people."

To discover what great differences Cleisthenes made in the government of Athens, we must look at what life was like before he gained control. We must return to the stony, mountainous country of Greece in the sixth century BC and find out how both ordinary people and important leaders lived and died and how their lives were governed. Then we should be able to understand something of the great changes made by Cleisthenes and how the process of democracy developed over the following centuries.

THE PHYSICAL ENVIRONMENT

Cleisthenes grew up and was educated in Greece, a land of mountains, islands, and seacoasts. Greece protrudes from the European continent out into the Mediterranean Sea. To the west of Greece is the Ionian Sea. To the east lies the Aegean Sea, which separated Greece from Asia Minor and the Persian Empire. The Gulf of Corinth divides the country in half, with the lower half called the Peloponnese and the upper half called the Greek mainland. Countless islands surround this peninsula. In ancient Greece there were some areas of fertile land, but these were few and far between. These fertile areas were separated from each other by the sea, steep mountains, or low, wooded hills.

The rivers that flowed through the plains of Greece flooded in winter, leaving reasonably fertile soil to support various crops. Patches of fertile soil on higher ground or hillsides were terraced to increase the area available for farming, but only one-fifth of Greek land could produce essential crops like cereals, olives, and grapes. For the majority of Greeks, farming was their job, and they were dependent on the land to survive. Grapes were harvested in September. Ploughing and sowing continued through October and November. In November, olives were gathered, just as they are still gathered today, with nets and sticks, and the grain harvest took place in May. The poet Hesiod wrote in the eighth century BC that farming was a hard business. Many years after Cleisthenes, another poet called Menander wrote:

A typical Attic farmer,
Struggling with rocks that yield nothing
  but savory and sage
And getting nothing out of it but aches
  and pains.

The land provided a few natural resources—limestone rock, high-quality marble near Attica (both used for building projects in the generations after Cleisthenes), clay, and timber. Clay was used to produce fired pottery, roof tiles, and bricks. Timber was used in large quantities for building projects and ships, and for burning as a fuel.

Greece enjoys a typical Mediterranean climate, intensely hot and dry in the summer, with intermittent but heavy rains in the winter. Late summer brings strong breezes, making navigation around the rugged coastlines even trickier. This mild and pleasant climate encouraged the ancient Greeks to spend much time outdoors. They had little need to stay inside for warmth and could easily hold meetings together in the open air. The philosopher Aristotle commented that the climate played a large part in making the Greeks behave as they did politically. He wrote that northern Europeans and those who

A view of the mountainous scenery of Attica, the countryside surrounding Athens

lived in cold climates were "full of energy but rather lacking in skill . . . and there-fore lack political organization." People in very hot countries, he wrote, had intellect and skill "but lack energy." He continued:

"But the people of Greece occupy a middle geographic position and so have both energy and intelligence. They retain their freedom and have the best political institutions. In fact if they could achieve unity they could control the rest of the world."

THE CITY-STATE

The regions where Greeks could survive on the few areas of good land were often cut off from each other by stretches of water or high mountains. For this reason, the communities that arose in ancient Greece were relatively small cities surrounded by farmland, and each city functioned as an independent state, with its citizens feeling an allegiance only to their city. There was no nation or empire known as Greece,

and no individual ruled over the entire peninsula. Between the many city-states, routes and roads were difficult to use, and throughout the winter months communication by land was virtually impossible. Travel by sea was more suitable in many cases, but even so it was difficult for one city-state to keep in regular contact with other city-states. Each city-state had its own traditions and customs. To look at a map of Greece, it would be easy to assume that in ancient times it was one united country. In fact, Greece in the time of Cleisthenes consisted of over 150 separate city-states. These city-states were all separate from each other, and the country as a whole had no central government.

The city-state was called a *polis*. From this ancient word, modern English derives the words "politics," "police," and "metropolitan." The polis was a single town or city set in farmland. The average territory of the polis extended over about 400 square miles, but the size of each

The ruins of the Acropolis, in the center of Athens

polis varied greatly. Some, like Athens and Sparta, were much larger than others. Cleisthenes' polis was Athens, which administered over 1,000 square miles of territory. Whatever its size, the polis mattered to the Greeks because they saw their cities as the places

where they belonged, just as we think of our country. The farmer in the countryside outside the city walls was as much a part of his polis as the jug maker in the town center. These city-states were just like small countries within the larger area called Greece.

All the Greeks did have some things in common. They used the same alphabet and the same language. They shared the same gods and read the same epic poems. At times, city-states would join together to fight a common enemy, and athletes from different city-states would meet to compete in the regularly held Olympic Games. Some city-states made alliances with each other, while others fought between themselves for economic or political reasons. The Greeks had developed this system during the two centuries before Cleisthenes, and it was within this structure of city-states that he grew up and eventually became a leader.

A vase painting of a symposium in progress. Symposia were drinking parties for young men.

ATHENS

Cleisthenes grew up in Athens and the area around Athens known as Attica. Like many ancient cities, Athens had an area of high ground called the *acropolis*, to which the population could flock in times of danger. Here there was a temple to Athene, the city's patron goddess.

In the center of Athens was the *agora*, an open area used as a marketplace and meeting area for public gatherings and announcements. Around the agora, in an unplanned arrangement, were all the houses and other buildings of the city. Very few Greek houses have survived, as only important public structures were made of stone, but archaeologists have discovered that the homes of wealthy Athenians like Cleisthenes were built around a central courtyard. Windows were small, water supplies came from a well or fountain, and burning charcoal or wood provided heat for cooking. The house would have had a bathroom with drainage to the outside and an altar situated in a prominent place. Women and men used separate areas of the house. The aristocratic women in Cleisthenes' family would have spent their days in the *gynaeceum,* weaving and managing the household slaves.

Another painting of a single young man at a symposium

The men used an *andron*, an elaborate room with the floor raised on all four sides for couches. Here, from his youth onward, someone like Cleisthenes would take part in *symposia*, drinking parties that were an

important part of aristocratic life. A symposium was an occasion for men to drink and socialize together, but with lots of customs and rules. The "president" of the occasion decided the mixture of wine and water in the large *krater*, the mixing bowl from which the men were served. Guests reclined on couches and cushions. Entertainment was provided by dancing girls, or a flute player would accompany the men as they sang drinking songs.

Athletic contests were extremely important to the aristocracy. The Greeks had four main festivals of games, all connected with religious shrines, to which contestants came from all over the Greek world. The Olympic and Delphic Games were held every four years, and the Nemean and Isthmian Games were held every two years. Each year, Cleisthenes would have attended at least one athletic competition. His family would have taken part in the four-horse chariot events, but other contests

A view of modern Athens with the Acropolis in the distance

involved running, the pentathlon, box-ing, and wrestling, all for the prize of a crown of laurel or olive leaves. The real reward for any victor in the games was in his home city where he would be showered with prizes and honors.

THE ATHENIAN POLITICAL SYSTEM

Each man in a polis had loyalties to three things—his family, his tribe, and the polis itself. Within each polis and within each tribe, there were some families who were more important than others. These families were the *eupatridae*, or "well-born," and they held most of the power. These noble families, who are often called aristocrats, frequently struggled between themselves to gain political power in their community. The aristocratic families were wealthy and controlled much of the land. Sometimes they were popular, but often they were not. The writer Hesiod in the eighth century BC described the nobles of his community as "gift-devouring."

As the Britons have their King Arthur, the ancient Athenians also had their legendary

23

A late sixth-century BC bronze helmet

founder. King Theseus is supposed to have ruled Athens in the Mycenean Age more than a thousand years before the birth of Christ. He brought together the people of Athens and the surrounding region of Attica. He provided the city with a central council for the local aristocrats to hold meetings. By the seventh century BC, there was no longer a single king in Athens. Instead, the polis was ruled by nine *archons*. The archons were chosen each year, and they were selected from the eupatridae. They were always men. Women had no place in Greek government. Athens was in effect ruled by just a few wealthy and influential families.

The job of the archons was to maintain order in the community, and they accomplished this in several ways. They supervised religious rituals, making sure that religious occasions were observed properly. They made decisions on behalf of the state and made sure that the military forces were adequate and would keep the state safe from attack. They kept the written laws of the state and made sure that everyone obeyed those laws. When a man had served his year as an archon, he then became a member of the *Areopagus*, so called because it would meet on the Areopagus, or "Hill of Ares," the god of war. The Areopagus was a sort of senate of senior aristocrats that had far-reaching powers. Every year this council chose who would become the next archons.

Most people in ancient Athens were poor farmers. They farmed at subsistence level. This means that they could grow just enough food for themselves and their families to survive. When a farmer's crops failed, he would obtain a loan from a wealthy landowner to buy food for his family and animals until the next harvest. If the next harvest also failed, he would be unable to pay back the loan from the previous year. Now the poor farmer would have to give up his land as payment for the loan and work for the wealthy landowner as a tenant, giving him half of the annual harvest.

A *clepsydra*, or water clock, used to measure the length of speeches in the Athenian court of justice

If the farmer was still unable to make ends meet, he had no choice but to give himself and his family in "debt-bondage" to the landowner. He now had to work the land for the landowner almost as a slave, with no real hope of ever repaying the original loan. His only other option was to leave his homeland and start a new life somewhere else. There was a large class of *hektemoroi*, men who had to give one-sixth of their produce to an overlord, which was a huge burden. Over time, just a few aristocratic families owned and controlled most of the land and wealth in Attica. This led to problems.

SOLON

In 594 BC, when the people of Athens—especially the poor—were very unhappy about the general state of affairs, a politician named Solon was given the power to try to improve the situation. He was an aristocrat, but in his younger days he had been poor and he understood the plight of those in debt. He is famous for the laws he made, which he wrote down in a poetic form so that people would remember them more easily. Many of Solon's measures were popular. He prevented merchants from selling grain abroad so that there was more food in Athens for the poor. He set up a new court to which people could appeal if they thought they had been wrongly judged. He also encouraged craftsmen from other parts of Greece to come to Athens and granted them Athenian citizenship. He made the Athenians use the same money as other Greek city-states, and this encouraged the development of trade and industry. But Solon's most important act was to cancel many debts, and he forbade those who were in debt, like the subsistence farmers in Attica, from being sold into slavery. Some Athenians who had been sent away or had fled from the city of Athens into exile because of debt were allowed to return home. The obligation of the hektemoroi was also abolished, and the land they farmed became their own.

Although he wrote these laws, Solon did not change the political organization of Athens greatly. He did set up a new council of 400 men called the *boule*. One hundred men from each of the four tribes of Attica sat on this council. He also allowed every adult male Athenian a place in the *ekklesia*, or Assembly, although we do not know what powers this assembly actually had. Solon thus gave a voice to the people, but he did not grant them real power. The 400 men in the boule probably decided what laws to present to the Assembly. The archons and the Areopagus remained the real center of political power.

THE TYRANNY OF PEISISTRATUS

Unfortunately, we do not know enough about the early life of Cleisthenes to describe how he grew up, how he was educated, or even if he married. We do not know his exact date of birth or even how and when he died. We do know that he was an aristocrat, a member of the prominent Alcmaeonidae family.

The Greek historian Herodotus tells several stories about the origin of the Alcmaeonidae family and Cleisthenes' ancestors that may or may not be true. One such story goes like this. King Croesus of Lydia was famous for his enormous wealth and vast fortune. He once sent some of his countrymen to Delphi in Greece. When they returned, they reported back to King Croesus and said that a man named Alcmaeon had given to them "all the assistance in his power."

The ruins of the Temple of Athena on the Greek island of Aegina

King Croesus invited this man Alcmaeon to Sardis in Lydia, and as a reward for his help, the king offered him as much gold as he could carry on his person at one time. Alcmaeon thought for a while and decided upon the best way to take advantage of this once-in-a-lifetime offer. He dressed himself in a large tunic that was loose and baggy at the front. On his feet he wore a pair of the widest top boots that he could find. Wearing this outfit, he followed the king's servants into the treasury. Here he attacked a heap of gold dust. He crammed handfuls of the precious gold into his boots, all the way up his legs until they were full. He filled the front of his tunic with gold dust, sprinkled it into his hair, and stuffed some into his mouth. Then he staggered out of the treasury, every single part of him bulging with gold. He was so heavy with the treasure that he could hardly drag one foot after the other. When King Croesus saw him he burst out laughing. The king was so amused that he gave Alcmaeon all the gold he was carrying and much more besides.

So Alcmaeon's family found themselves extremely wealthy, and Alcmaeon decided to spend some of his newfound riches on racehorses with which he was able to win the prestigious chariot race at Olympia. Alcmaeon and his descendants were known as the Alcmaeonidae, and Cleisthenes was a member of this aristocratic family. True or not, the story indicates that the family was considered extremely wealthy.

THE CURSE

There is another story told about the Alcmaeonidae that reflects their deep involvement in the politics of Athens. At the time of Cleisthenes' birth, his family was still affected by a curse that had been placed upon Megacles, Cleisthenes' great-grandfather.

Around 630 BC, when Megacles was the chief archon in Athens, an Athenian nobleman called Cylon tried to become the tyrant, or supreme leader, of the city. He tried to take control of Athens from the Acropolis, the highest point of the city. This attempt to gain power failed, and Cylon and his friends fled for their lives and sought safety at an altar. Normally, a Greek citizen could remain in a temple or at an altar, claiming the protection of a Greek god and remaining safe until the situation could be resolved.

Cylon's friends heard that their lives would be spared if they left their place of sanctuary, so they emerged and handed themselves over to the officials in Athens. However, someone broke

The ruins of the
Temple of Apollo at
Delphi

the agreement and they were all put to death. Because Megacles was the man in charge at the time, the blame for this fell on him. Advice from the Oracle at Delphi said that a curse should be put on all the Alcmaeonidae. The entire family had to leave Athens and go into exile, something they would have to do again years later. People remembered this curse, and the enemies of Cleisthenes' family used it to attack the Alcmaeonidae many times over the next 200 years.

Herodotus tells another story about Cleisthenes' grandfather, who was also called Cleisthenes, and Cleisthenes' father, who was also called Megacles. Herodotus refers to the grandfather as Cleisthenes of Sicyon. Cleisthenes of Sicyon had a daughter named Agarista, and he wanted to marry her off to the best man in the whole of Greece. During the Olympic Games, in which he had won a chariot race, he had a public announcement made. Any Greek who wanted to have the chance to

An artist's reconstruction of an Athenian bathhouse

marry his daughter had to come to Sicyon within sixty days. Cleisthenes of Sicyon then announced that he would choose a husband for his daughter one year later, when he had had a good chance to get to know them all. He built a race track and a wrestling ring, and soon the

finest young men came from all over Greece to try to impress him and gain the hand of his daughter. Herodotus describes some of the contenders who wanted the chance to be the son-in-law of someone as wealthy and powerful as Cleisthenes of Sicyon. The suitors included Smindyrides, "a man noted for delicate and luxurious living," Males, "brother of the strongest man in Greece," and Hippocleides, "the wealthiest and best looking man in Greece."

Cleisthenes of Sicyon spent the full year living with these men in his house. He found out as much about each of them as he could. He tested them to discover what kind of parents they had and how well educated they seemed. He watched how they performed in the gymnasia and made note of their personal qualities and good manners. The most important test of all was how they behaved at the dinner table. Toward the end of this long trial, it seemed that two men,

An artist's reconstruction of the Bouleuterion (right foreground), seat of the Boule, the Athenian assembly.

both from Athens, had become his favorites: Hippocleides, the wealthiest, and Megacles, whose father, Alcmaeon, had been enriched by King Croesus.

At last, when the day came to announce his choice, Cleisthenes of Sicyon made a large sacrifice to the gods of a hundred oxen, and he arranged a spectacular feast for all the suitors and many other people from his lands. After dinner, the suitors showed off and talked and sang to entertain and impress the guests. So far, Hippocleides seemed the best, and Cleisthenes of Sicyon had virtually made his final decision. However, as the evening went on, Hippocleides drank more and more wine. He called for a flute player and started to dance to the music. Cleisthenes of Sicyon began to feel uneasy about his choice of son-in-law. His doubts became stronger when Hippocleides called for a table and began to dance on the top of it. After several dances, Hippocleides became even more adventurous and stood on his head on the table waving his legs in the air in time to the music.

Cleisthenes of Sicyon was furious. He shouted out to Hippocleides, "You have danced away your marriage!" In reply, Hippocleides called out cheerfully, "I could hardly care less." So Cleisthenes of Sicyon announced that his other favorite, Megacles, was to be given the hand of his daughter Agarista in marriage, and all the other suitors were each paid a large amount of money as compensation for their year spent away from home. Presumably, the curse on the Alcmaeonidae did not concern Cleisthenes of Sicyon when he chose Megacles as a son-in-law. Megacles and Agarista were married and had a son, and they named him Cleisthenes.

Cleisthenes led a privileged existence in a society where life was hard, especially for women and slaves and poor farmers. He was undoubtedly educated and trained as someone from an important family, and he must have realized that he was destined for a life of influence at some level in his society. As an aristocrat, Cleisthenes knew that one day he would be a military leader. Greek soldiers provided their own armor, which was very expensive. Rich nobles could therefore be extremely powerful on the battlefield since they were the best armed and trained. They commanded all those who were linked to them: family members, lesser nobles, rich farmers, and tenants. Soldiers in the Greek infantry were called *hoplites*.

CONFLICT

After the reign of Solon, when Cleisthenes was in his twenties, there was trouble. The Alcmaeonidae had returned to Athens from exile before 594 BC, and they were great supporters of Solon. But not all Athenians approved of Solon's reforms. The only people who still had real power to rule were the well-born, aristocratic families, through their membership in the Areopagus. These important families—and Cleisthenes' family was one of them—were always arguing and disagreeing and fighting over the leadership of the polis. Following Solon's reforms this feuding continued. The Athenians were divided into three main groups. There were the *paralia*, or the

A painting on an amphora, or large storage jar, of a cithara player

"men of the shore." The paralia were mostly middle-class traders, sailors, and fishermen, as well as poor peasants, who wanted Solon's reforms. Their leader was Megacles, Cleisthenes' father. His family had farms south of the city of Athens, near the sea. There were also the *pedion*, or the "men of the plain," who were mostly the eupatridae, or aristocrats. They were rich landowners in the most fertile areas of Attica who wanted to rule Athens in their own interests. Their leader was Lycurgus. Finally, there were the *diacria*, the "men of the hill." They were led by an aristocrat called Peisistratus, who wanted power for himself. These men were small hill farmers, shepherds, and many of the people in the city of Athens.

The paralia were made up mostly of those who lived in the area southeast of Athens, and this was the country stronghold of the Alcmaeonidae family. Their leader, Megacles, Cleisthenes' father, disagreed with Lycurgus and the pedion. The aristocratic families in this party lost much wealth under the rulings of Solon, and they wanted it back, but Megacles and his supporters knew that a great disparity in the wealth held by different classes of Athenians would lead to political chaos. As the son of an aristocratic leader, Cleisthenes must have gained valuable insights from observing his father's activities during this period of time.

TYRANNY

Some Greeks became very wealthy by being successful farmers or traders. Yet they could not become rulers because they were not aristocrats. Some men must have resented this and realized that there were other ways of gaining power and influence. All Athenian men had to be prepared to fight for their state and were expected to join the army when required. The more wealthy the man, the more armor and equipment he had to provide. As men trained together to become hoplites, or infantrymen, they must have become aware that a citizen could be very powerful if he could command an army. In several communities, men emerged who had not only wealth but the support of armed soldiers. Such men were in a position to seize absolute power by force. Such a leader was known as a tyrant.

The word "tyrant" has changed its meaning since the ancient Greeks invented it. Today we describe a tyrant as a ruler who uses power oppressively. Aristotle tells us that a tyrant was not necessarily like this in ancient Greece. Instead, a tyrant was someone who had taken power "unconstitutionally," that is, someone who had not gone through the proper channels of government and who made the laws without consultation with any other political group. In many cases, such men came to power with popular programs and widespread support among the poorer classes, who were willing to promote a tyrant to break the power of the oligopoly, the aristocrats who chose the archons. In ancient Greek history, the tyrant often became the transitional figure leading to a more democratic state. Aristotle wrote that a tyrant who has generally good motives can make a good ruler, being

> a king and a guardian of the house . . . entrusted with the affairs of others, aiming not at excess in all that relates to living but at moderation, one who makes friends with the leading citizens, but is also the people's leader.

Solon had been such a tyrant. He had been appointed chief archon and had been given sole power, more or less, for a year to sort out the difficult economic situation in Athens. But the political situation in Athens remained very unsettled after Solon. The aristocracy wanted their old privileges back. The poor wanted even more reforms. And the group led by Cleisthenes' family wanted a middle way. Now the struggle between the various political factions in Athens would produce another tyrant, Peisistratus, but not without a struggle first against, among others, Megacles, father of Cleisthenes.

Peisistratus was a military hero who garnered support from many in the poorer classes. With their help, he made three attempts to take control of Athens. Two of

these attempts involved trickery. Herodotus describes the first attempt in 561 BC:

> Peisistratus . . . coming forward as the champion of the "men of the hill," devised a plan as follows: he made cuts on his own body and into the skin of his mules. Then he drove his cart into the market square and pretended that he had escaped from his enemies, who tried to kill him as he was driving out of town. Then, relying on the military reputation he had won during his command of the expedition against Megara . . . he asked the assembly to give him armed soldiers for protection.

The Athenians were taken in by this trick. Peisistratus used the armed guard given to him by the Athenians to take control of the Acropolis and thus make himself the supreme leader of Athens. Peisistratus did not last long as leader this first time. Megacles, Cleisthenes' father, and Lycurgus joined their forces and threw Peisistratus out of Athens. For a while, Megacles and Lycurgus had joint control of the state, but their partnership was not successful. The two men could not work together, and Megacles was frustrated by the situation. So Megacles himself devised a plan to bring Peisistratus back to power, perhaps hoping to share power with Peisistratus rather than Lycurgus, as their political views were more alike.

In Peisistratus's second attempt to gain power in 556 BC, Megacles decided that he would offer his daughter, Cleisthenes' sister, as a wife to Peisistratus. The idea was that the two families would be united by blood and both could rule Athens. Although Peisistratus would be in charge, Megacles would be influential because he would be related to Peisistratus, and when children were born they would have common heirs. Megacles and Peisistratus needed a dramatic way of convincing the people to accept Peisistratus, and they thought up another plan.

It seems that they thought that the best way would be to appeal to the Athenians' religious side. Peisistratus found a very tall woman called Phye who came from the village of Paeania. Megacles and Peisistratus dressed her up to look like the goddess Athene, the patron of Athens, wearing a suit of armor. They stood her on a chariot and asked her to stand in an impressive pose. Then they drove into Athens. They had sent messengers ahead of them to announce that the Athenians should welcome Peisistratus back because the goddess Athene herself was bringing him home to the Acropolis, where her temple was. Rumors spread all over the city and the surrounding countryside. Herodotus says that "both villagers and townspeople were convinced that the woman really was the goddess and offered her their prayers and received Peisistratus with open arms."

Herodotus described this event as "the silliest trick ever." He wrote that the Athenians were not idiots, but had "superior wits" and "of all the Greeks the Athenians are allowed to be the most intelligent." But perhaps it may have been that at the time of Peisistratus they were more trusting and devout, and the poor who constituted Peisistratus's main supporters were certainly less sophisticated and less educated.

Peisistratus married Cleisthenes' sister, but things started to go wrong fairly quickly. Because of the Alcmaeonidae curse and because he had grown children from his earlier marriage, Peisistratus did not want to have children with his new wife. Cleisthenes' sister told her mother that Peisistratus was not a proper husband and that he had no wish to have children. Megacles was furious. Without common heirs, Megacles' influence with Peisistratus would be minimal. Megacles turned his back on Peisistratus, and working with the other nobles, Megacles was able to have Peisistratus sent away.

Peisistratus left Athens for ten years, until 546 BC, when he again tried to take control of the city-state. During this time in exile, Peisistratus went to Eretria and devised a plan with the help of his sons. The family spent the time assembling a mercenary army. Mercenaries are soldiers who fight for any cause as long as they are paid well enough. Peisistratus went to live miles away from Athens in the northern region between Macedon and Thrace, where there were gold and silver mines. Here they extracted these precious metals and gained great wealth.

Peisistratus built ships and persuaded Scythian archers to fight for him. Some other Greek city-states supported Peisistratus. In fact, he was the recipient of massive foreign aid—Thessalian mercenaries, troops from Eretria, and support from Lygdamis, the tyrant of Naxos. Eventually, when they were ready, Peisistratus's army marched to attack Athens.

The Athenians, who according to Herodotus had not taken much notice of Peisistratus while he was out of the country, now had to assemble their army. The Athenians met Peisistratus's army face-to-face in the land between Athens and Marathon. Some of the oppressed farmers and poorer countrymen of Attica must have gone to join Peisistratus's army when they realized that their popular leader was trying to return. Peisistratus's soldiers proved to be the stronger force, and the Athenians fled in small groups, most returning to their homes. Herodotus paints a pathetic picture of Athens at the time of the battle. Just as Peisistratus gave the order to advance on the city, the Athenians inside were having lunch, and others were having an afternoon nap or playing dice after their meal. So Peisistratus's army

Washing basins used to separate silver ore at the silver mines near Laurium in southern Attica

met with no resistance in the city. Peisistratus gained unchallenged power in Athens, and he and his family were to rule for the next thirty-six years. It was now the turn of Cleisthenes and his family to go into exile.

LIFE IN EXILE

In the ancient world, where there were few legal codes or provisions for political retirement, the most expedient thing to do with political opponents was to have them removed, either through execution or exile. The Athenians in particular had instituted the system of exile, sending undesirable individuals out of the city. Life outside the polis meant a loss of belonging, a loss of rights, and for many a loss of income and security. Exiles had to find a new way of life away from the polis, until such time as they were invited back or seized the opportunity to return. The risks of returning when not welcome involved a hostile reception and possible assassination, so exile was taken seriously. Exile literally means an enforced absence or banishment from home, and this was the state in which the young man Cleisthenes and his family found themselves.

Cleisthenes and his family may have lost some of their property, or it may have been managed for them in their absence by supporters or relatives. But for most Athenians the period of Peisistratus's tyranny and the Alcmaeonidae's exile brought some peace and stability after years of feuding and factionalism. Now many farmers could farm their land and harvest their wheat, vines, and olives without interruption. Peisistratus, in fact, tried to reinforce the reforms of Solon and extend more political power to the poorer classes by giving more authority to the Assembly and reforming the court system. In the end, historians would decide that his tyranny and the restrictions he imposed on aristocratic power were necessary to the development of Athenian democracy.

For those who were exiled, however, this could be a time to regroup and plan their return. This is what Peisistratus did during his ten-year exile, and it seems that the Alcmaeonidae family also put their time in exile to good use. As nothing is heard of Megacles after 546 BC, when the Alcmaeonidae fled Attica, it is likely that during Peisistratus's rule in Athens, Megacles died. Now Cleisthenes

A fifth-century BC carving of a lion hunt

was the head of the family. It appears that Cleisthenes and his relatives took refuge in Delphi. Delphi is a small village in the foothills of Mount Parnassus with stunning views and scenery. Here, from the seventh century onward, there were temples, treasuries, an athletics stadium, and the famous Temple of Apollo where people came to hear prophecies about the future. The Alcmaeonidae are mentioned several times in connection with Delphi. When in an earlier time a people called the Criseans claimed control of the famous shrine at Delphi and took money from everyone who visited there, Cleisthenes' two grandfathers, Alcmaeon and Cleisthenes of Sicyon, fought together to free Delphi from the Criseans.

In 548 BC, the Temple of Apollo at Delphi was destroyed by fire. Those who looked after Delphi and maintained the temple were called the Amphictyonic Council. The council decided that the temple had to be rebuilt, and the contract for completing this rebuilding was awarded to Cleisthenes and his family. This contract gave Cleisthenes the chance to administer and disburse huge sums of money, which he did with efficiency and honesty. Cleisthenes impressed the people of Delphi and the Amphictyonic Council by using his own family wealth to add better features to the temple. Instead of the local building stone, Cleisthenes had marble brought from Paria to adorn the front of the temple. The cost of rebuilding the temple was 300 talents, an enormous fortune to spend on one building, and donations were made by people from all over the Greek world and Egypt. This task earned Cleisthenes some very important friends and allies.

ATHENS UNDER PEISISTRATUS

The Athenian constitution, written by one of Aristotle's pupils, emphasizes the popularity of Peisistratus's rule. He established peaceful relations with most of the other Greek city-states. His own personal fortune was maintained from his mining interests in the north, and it is thought that he also developed the silver mines at Laurium, which kept the city of Athens on a very solid financial basis. Most important of all, he preserved and extended the reforms of Solon and curtailed the power of the aristocrats. The mercenary army of Scythian archers and others that Peisistratus had relied upon to seize power now became the state's first independent police force, and this put an end to the gangs and private armies

A terra-cotta figure
of a seated scribe

maintained by the nobles. It was no longer necessary for citizens to bear arms as they moved about the streets of Athens.

Peisistratus created a system of traveling judges, both to alleviate congestion in the city courts and to bring justice into rural areas, where wealthy landowners had previously dominated the courts. He instituted a tax on agricultural produce and used the revenue to provide loans to peasant farmers. In some cases, he took away the land of aristocrats who were political opponents and distributed the land to those who actually farmed it. He began a number of public works programs, employing people to build aqueducts, roads, and buildings. Giving land to the landless and work to the unemployed reduced the number of vagrants who wandered the streets of Athens, contributing to a sense of public safety.

Changes like this enforced the authority of the central government and helped to make it appear independent of the local aristocrats. Peisistratus created a more prosperous and politically stable state, and this created the foundation for the later democratic reforms of Cleisthenes. Believing that religious and cultural institutions were essential to the unity of the state, Peisistratus also increased the importance of Athenian religious festivals. He built a new temple to Athene on the Acropolis and expanded the Panathenaia, the great religious festival held every year that attracted people from all over Greece. He promoted poetry readings and organized the first attempt to write down the epic poems of Homer so that the *Iliad* and the *Odyssey* could be read out loud at the Panathenaia. Until this time, the poems had been passed on for generations by bards who recited the lines from memory. Peisistratus also promoted athletic competitions and offered the winners commemorative painted vases filled with olive oil. Craftsmen were brought to Athens from all over Greece, and the arts flourished. Peisistratus ruled until his death in 527 BC. Herodotus describes him this way:

> He was no revolutionary, but governed the country in an orderly and excellent manner, without changing the laws or disturbing the existing magistracies.

RETURN FROM EXILE

After Peisistratus's death, his power passed on to his two sons, Hippias and Hipparchus. Cleisthenes and his family returned to Athens at some point either late during the reign of Peisistratus or that of his sons. The Alcmaeonidae family were definitely settled back in Athens when Hippias inherited the leadership from his father. Perhaps as Hippias took over he wanted to reconcile himself with those aristocrats who had gone into exile. He wanted their support and favor so that they would not turn against him later on. An inscription found in the agora, the Athenian marketplace, even lists Cleisthenes as one of the archons for the year 525 BC. At the age of about forty-five, this was probably Cleisthenes' first taste of power in the city of Athens.

Peisistratus had made enemies of many of the aristocrats during his reign, and his son inherited their resentments. Two young aristocrats named Harmodius and Aristogeiton decided to take drastic action. At the Panathenaia festival in 514 BC, they planned to kill Hipparchus, Peisistratus's son and Hippias's brother. Herodotus tells us that the night before the Panathenaia, Hipparchus had a vivid dream that warned him of danger. The following day Harmodius and Aristogeiton waited to catch Hippias on the Acropolis as he was about to receive the great procession that was part of the festival. A misunderstanding delayed the

A bronze figure of a discus thrower

arrival of all the conspirators, but without waiting for their accomplices Harmodius and Aristogeiton lurched toward Hipparchus and stabbed him. A bodyguard killed Harmodius straight away. Aristogeiton was caught and tortured for a long time. Under torture, he gave the names of several other young aristocrats involved in the plot, and finally Hippias himself killed Aristogeiton with his dagger, taking revenge for his brother's death.

This murderous event changed everything. Hippias now feared for his life and became suspicious and withdrawn. His reign became harsh and cruel. Hippias knew that he had enemies and needed protection. He assembled a personal bodyguard of mercenary soldiers and increased everyone's taxes to pay for them. During the following years, he began to lose his grip on power.

When it became clear that Hippias was becoming increasingly unpopular and about to lose his leadership, some aristocrats, including Cleisthenes, decided to make their move. They joined forces and fought Hippias's men in a battle at a place called Leipsydrium near Mt. Parnes. They lost the conflict, and a great many noble young men were killed. Cleisthenes and

his allies then realized that they needed more help to overthrow Hippias.

Cleisthenes' popularity in Delphi for rebuilding the Temple of Apollo when he had been in exile now proved to be of crucial importance. He bribed the Delphic oracle to tell every Spartan who came to the city that it was their duty to free Athens from tyranny. The words of the Delphic oracle were not to be taken lightly anywhere in Greece, and Cleisthenes had decided that he needed the Spartan army to overthrow Hippias.

Sparta was a city-state in the southeast of the Peloponnese, the southern part of Greece separated from the mainland by the Gulf of Corinth. The Spartans were quite different from the Athenians, and the harsh and ordered way of life in Sparta has led to the modern English meaning of the word "spartan" as simple, frugal, and without luxury. Spartan children were taken from their mothers at the age of seven and sent to military school. There they experienced extreme hardship and discipline. The whole educational system aimed to encourage endurance and courage and military skills. Marriage was allowed at the age of twenty, but men still had to live together in barracks until they were thirty. The Spartans conquered the peoples around them and made many of them slaves; each Spartan had an allocation of land that was farmed for him by the slaves, who were called helots. The Spartans' military training, in fact, was to produce an army capable of keeping the slaves in check. This military existence left little time for literature, art, or the building of fine cities. The Spartans did not even build city walls, believing that soldiers would fight more bravely if they realized that there were no defensive works to hide behind. So the Spartans had a city-state with the most powerful army in Greece. Whereas the Athenian men had only to serve in the army for two years, each Spartan trained as a soldier for twenty-three years. It was this strong, fighting force that Cleisthenes needed to remove Hippias.

The king of Sparta at that time was called Cleomenes. Each time Cleomenes sent a Spartan to the Oracle at Delphi, Herodotus tells us that this message was given to him: "First free Athens." Cleomenes and the Spartans did not like tyrants anyway. They had fought to remove tyrants from other parts of Greece. The Spartans may have been genuinely taken in by the Oracle at Delphi and believed that the gods were instructing them to take this particular course of action. But Cleomenes knew that if Athens was returned to the rule of the aristocracy, then goodwill would be shown to Sparta and some powerful and useful alliances might be formed in the future.

The Spartans first sent a group under the command of Anchimolius to attack Hippias by sea, but they were defeated. Whatever the virtues of the Spartan army, the Athenians had the better navy. Then Cleomenes himself took a much larger army by land and joined with the Athenian exiles. The Athenian exiles were led by Cleisthenes and another aristocrat, Isagoras, the son of Tisander. We do not know much about Isagoras except that he was from an old, noble family. He was a friend of the Spartan king and he was a political rival of Cleisthenes'. For now, Cleisthenes and Isagoras

A relief carving of a
woman with a child

were united in trying to defeat Hippias. Their motives and political views, however, were very different. Isagoras represented the traditional aristocracy. Cleisthenes was soon to show that he had new and radical ideas.

The Spartans attacked Athens in 510 BC, and Hippias took refuge behind the walls of the Acropolis. Hippias tried to send his children to safety, but they were captured and held hostage. To save his children, Hippias surrendered. Within five days, he and his followers had left the country for exile in Persia, and the Spartans returned home.

CLEISTHENES AND ISAGORAS

Once Hippias was gone, the two men competing for control of Athens were Cleisthenes and Isagoras. They struggled with each other for two years. Isagoras was on very good terms with Cleomenes, the Spartan king. Herodotus, writing like a gossip columnist, even goes so far as to say that when Cleomenes stayed at Isagoras's house, he was much too friendly with Isagoras's wife! Isagoras also had lots of supporters among the aristocrats in Athens, and in 508 BC, he gained great power when he was chosen archon.

A painting on the outside of a bowl that shows women with flowers and perfume flasks

Cleisthenes began to suggest changes in the social divisions in Athens and new ways of organizing political power. His ideas for a new way of government were gaining approval in the Athenian Assembly. These new ideas were not at all popular with Isagoras, who called on Cleomenes to come and help expel Cleisthenes from Athens. Cleomenes demanded the expulsion of "those under the curse of the Alcmaeonidae," and the Spartans arrived in Athens in force. Cleisthenes could do nothing when faced with so many Spartan hoplites, and so he was forced to flee Athens along with 700 other families. He was in exile again.

The Spartans found 300 men who supported Isagoras and gave the government to them. The boule, the council that had run Athens, was abolished. This action shocked the Athenian people. The council members refused to obey orders to disperse. The Athenians picked up their weapons and angrily rose up against the Spartans and in fact trapped them behind the walls of the Acropolis, just as Hippias had been trapped there. After just two days, a truce was called and the Spartans left Athens. Many men who had fought for Isagoras with the Spartans on the Acropolis were taken prisoner and executed. Isagoras was powerless. Then Cleisthenes and the other families finally returned to Athens. At last Cleisthenes was in power and his reforms could begin.

Cleisthenes in Power

In 508 BC, when Cleisthenes was about sixty-two years old, his long-awaited chance for leadership had come. He began to restore the democratic aspects of the government of Solon and instituted far-reaching reforms that would permanently reduce the power of the aristocrats.

Cleisthenes' first major reform was to reorganize the Athenian tribal system. The four existing tribes were replaced by ten new tribes named for local heroes. The old tribes had come under the control of the aristocratic families. Each new tribe was composed of smaller political units called *demes*, which were organized geographically. A deme might correspond to a rural village or a district or neighborhood of the city. In the past, to be an Athenian citizen, you had to trace your lineage back to one of the original founding families of Athens. Now any adult male member of a deme could claim citizenship and participate in the governing bodies of the city. It is from the word deme that we derive the term "democracy."

Now, instead of belonging to an ancient tribe and obeying the aristocratic families who led that tribe, every Athenian belonged to a village or a deme. Scholars think that Cleisthenes created 139 demes. Athenian citizens in the demes could now assemble together and make their own decisions about matters that affected them. They could elect their own officials and were responsible for carrying out the laws of the central government. Each village kept its own money in a local treasury. The main official in charge of each village was called the *demarch*.

Each deme also kept its own list or register of citizens. Once a male Athenian reached the age of eighteen, he was given the status of citizenship and gained the right to vote and speak in the deme assembly. When there were disputes about who could or could not become a citizen of Athens, they were dealt with in the demes by the local leaders. Athenian citizenship was hereditary. This meant that from the

A terra-cotta figure
of an old woman
holding a baby

time of Cleisthenes onward, a man could be a citizen if he could prove that his father was a citizen. Record keeping in the demes became very important, and men were listed as follows: "Megacles, son of Hippocrates, from Alopeke." This example is taken from a broken pot found in Athens. An Athenian's name included his father's name and his deme name *(demotikon)* even if he moved to live in another deme. Cleisthenes wanted citizens to have the power to make decisions about government from the lowest level of society to the highest. Now no aristocratic Athenian could give or take away someone's citizenship. This was something a man gained for himself. His citizenship did not depend on wealth or connections or military power. It depended on his parentage. As long as his father was a citizen, then so was he.

The ten new tribes themselves, formed from the demes, were divided up in a manner that prevented any one tribe from occupying a single geographical area. Within each tribe, there were citizens from the city itself, from the coastal areas, and from the inland areas. This reorganization was designed to ensure that each tribe consisted of a mixture of classes of people—rich and poor, both large and small landowners, the educated and the

A vase painting of women
engaged in spinning

illiterate, and country folk and city dwellers. All this further reduced the influence of regional voting blocks controlled by local aristocrats. By mixing everyone up like this, Cleisthenes tried to create a body of citizens who could work together and who would not fall out into groups squabbling for power.

Apparently Cleisthenes himself drew up the first full list of Athenian citizens. He may also have created this list to show how many foreigners were living in Athens, so that supporters of the tyrants from other city-states could be removed and sent into exile. The Athenian army was also reorganized into ten regiments. Each of the ten tribes had to provide a regiment full of hoplite soldiers, a squadron of horsemen, and a general to command them. The ten generals were elected every year and could be reelected many times. Each man served in the army for two years. Cleisthenes introduced this measure to replace the old aristocratic system of military leadership and to limit the power of the noble families.

THE COUNCIL OF FIVE HUNDRED

Cleisthenes also created the boule, a new assembly of 500 members, to work alongside the old Assembly, which was a large body including all free Athenians. This Council of Five Hundred was made up of ordinary Athenian citizens. Ten times a year the names of fifty men over thirty years of age from each tribe were chosen by lot. Each lot of fifty men was called a *prytany*, and one prytany sat in council at any one time. A new group of fifty took over about every month. No citizen was allowed to sit on the council more than two times. This meant that most citizens of Athens probably had the chance to be on the council and make decisions at some point. Each day a different citizen from the prytany was put in charge of the council, and this man was chosen by lot.

Choosing council members and council leaders randomly by lot rather than by majority vote may seem odd to us today, but it eliminated the old Athenian system in which the

A terra-cotta figure of a seated woman stirring the contents of a cooking pot

most educated and eloquent speakers, usually nobles, could sway the citizens to vote for them. It was therefore another restriction on rule by the most powerful and richest men in the community. And with an assembly that would, over time, include most of the citizens, the randomness of the process was not an obstacle to good government.

Cleisthenes' council was designed to be democratic. On each day, the fifty Athenian citizens running the country would be from a cross section of society, from all walks of life and with different financial backgrounds. This method of choosing lawmakers aimed to ensure that no one person or group of people could gain too much power. Anyone who was becoming "too big for his boots," or who suggested an extreme course of action, would just be outvoted by the other members of the council. Every man could have his say in the government of Athens. In an effort to secure his own position over that of the old aristocratic groups led by his rival Isagoras, Cleisthenes had placed his trust in the broad support of the Athenian majority. The result was the first government by the people.

Cleisthenes also arranged for a new council house to be built in the agora, the marketplace of Athens, a permanent building that symbolized for everyone the long-term purpose of his reforms. The council that met here became the main ruling body in the city-state of Athens. Its job was to prepare laws for the larger Assembly of citizens, to put into practice decisions made by that Assembly, and to oversee all the magistrates. There were some decisions that this new council could not make. The boule could not declare war or send Athenian citizens into battle. That was the job of the Assembly. And the council could not make major recommendations or changes without the approval of the Assembly.

THE ASSEMBLY

Every citizen had the right to speak and vote at the Assembly. This large gathering of citizens met about once every ten days, and the Assembly soon found a new meeting place on a hill called the Pnyx. In about 500 BC, a platform terrace was carved out of the rock on this hill. On this terrace was the *bema,* or "speaker's stone," and the man speaking to the gathered crowd stood on this. Any citizen over twenty years old could stand on the bema and present his point of view to those sitting along

the hillside. As the years went by, it became possible for ordinary men who were good at public speaking to have a huge influence over this Assembly, even though they had no official position as leaders. Members of the boule stood here to present the decisions the Council of Five Hundred had made, and they would ask the Assembly to vote for or against the proposals. Each man raised his hand to vote, and the leaders and everyone else could see who held the majority.

The archons were still elected from the aristocracy, and these archons were the highest officials in the city-state. So there was still the opportunity for members of the upper classes to gain honor, prestige, and power in public life. In fact, for many years after Cleisthenes' reforms, the aristocracy still had great influence. The Areopagus was also retained by Cleisthenes. The Areopagus was the group of men who had once served as archons. Gradually, over a long time, the power of the men in the Areopagus declined until their only remaining power was to try murderers.

OSTRACISM

Another invention of Cleisthenes was ostracism. If a leader, or any individual who had political power, became too strong or behaved badly, the citizens of Athens could

Examples of ostraka, broken shards of pottery upon which Athenian citizens wrote the names of those they wished to ostracize, or exile, from the city for a period of ten years. One shard features the name of Aristeides, ostracized in 482 BC.

vote to send him into exile for a ten-year period. The man being ostracized would not lose his money, property, or citizenship, but he could be safely removed. Cleisthenes believed that this would prevent a repetition of the power struggle that he had had with Isagoras. Each year the men of the Assembly decided whether they wanted to send someone into exile. Each man took a piece of broken pottery called an *ostrakon*. On the piece of broken pottery, the man wrote the name of the leader who he thought should be sent away for the safety of Athens. These ostraka were dropped into a large pot and any person who had 6,000 votes against him was banished.

Though individuals had been exiled before, including Cleisthenes himself, the system of ostracism was not used until after Cleisthenes died. The first ostracism happened in 487 BC when one of Peisistratus's relatives, Hipparchus, son of Charmus of Collytus, was sent away. It was quite rare for ostracisms to take place, and only about ten men were ever ostracized by the people of Athens. However, the system was another example of Cleisthenes' desire to hand the power for such decisions to the people.

ISONOMIA

Cleisthenes created the essentials of the Athenian system of democratic government that continued almost unchanged for the next 200 years. But the Athenians did not call their political system "democracy." Before Cleisthenes, the ideal society in the eyes of men like Solon was something called *eunomia*, a Greek word that means "good order." For the political system he established, Cleisthenes used the word *isonomia*, which means "equal order." This system was very different from the concept of democracy as we know it today, but it was the beginning of a new political system that worked. Cleisthenes spread power more evenly across his society, and he gave individuals the chance to have a direct role in the rule of their society.

After 508 BC, we hear nothing more about Cleisthenes. All of a sudden, the little information that we have about him just dries up. Possibly he died, or he may have become very unpopular. One theory is that after his reforms, when the people of the city-states of Sparta, Chalcis, and Boetia became hostile to Athens and began to attack the city-state, Cleisthenes sent some officials to Persia for help. The Persians were the enemies of the Greeks, and if it was thought that Cleisthenes' messengers were forming an alliance with the Persians, Cleisthenes would have been in trouble. But we do not know this for sure.

We may never know Cleisthenes' motives for introducing this new way of government to Athens. If he introduced this system of isonomia to protect himself and to make his family powerful, then he failed. We do not hear much of the Alcmaeonidae again, except when they later became very unpopular. Cleisthenes probably was very unpopular with many of the aristocrats who lost their power.

Cleisthenes simply slips quietly out of the history books. His new ideas remained, and 2,500 years later we enjoy the benefits of democracy. Our democracy today is very different from the Greek system that developed in the years after Cleisthenes. We vote for representatives who make decisions on our behalf. The Athenians had developed a system of direct democracy, which meant that all citizens could vote on almost every decision. Imagine that today, in order to declare war on another nation, all our citizens had to vote in a special election before war could be declared. Imagine that our senators and representatives were chosen by lottery. That would be the Athenian way.

A fifth-century BC perfume jug with a painting of a hare

Another difference is that in Athens only free male citizens were eligible to vote. Women, slaves, and foreigners took no part in the process of government.

We have much for which to thank Cleisthenes and the Athenian people. Because of Cleisthenes, ordinary Athenians took a much more active part in public life. Because of Cleisthenes, the Athenians developed a democracy that worked and made their city strong.

Over the centuries, many people have been so convinced of the benefits of democracy that they, too, have been prepared to fight and struggle for this system. Of course, the idea of freedom and the participation of the people in government, as powerful as that idea is, does not guarantee that such a political system can always triumph over some form of tyranny. By 338 BC, Philip of Macedon had conquered Athens and the rest of Greece and absorbed it into his growing empire. The independent Greek city-state ceased to exist. But the historical record has preserved enough knowledge about early Greek democracy to have influenced the founding fathers of our own nation as they carried out their revolution and struggled to establish a government of the people, by the people, and for the people.

HOW DO WE KNOW?

The historian Herodotus was the first Greek to write a long prose work describing the events of the past, and this earned him the reputation, to quote the Roman writer Cicero, as the "father of history." Herodotus has also been accused by many scholars of being the "father of lies." The fact is that Herodotus wrote down many

A relief carving of close combat between two Greek warriors

stories that are entertaining and sometimes hard to believe. Herodotus was born in 484 BC in Halicarnassus in Asia Minor, now Bodrum in Turkey. He lived at a time when Athens was becoming powerful. His work is an organized and serious attempt to record the oral traditions about the past. This meant that he listened carefully to people and recorded their accounts of past events. Many of his sources were educated Greeks from the upper classes and wealthy members of society. These informants may have been biased, or just plain wrong. But Herodotus passed down the information in a clear and simple style, and the evidence is presented for us to believe or disbelieve as we see fit.

It is in Books 5 and 6 of his *History* that Herodotus gives us our information about Cleisthenes' family and the situation in Athens when Cleisthenes was alive. We must assume that the people who told Herodotus about Cleisthenes and his family were distant relatives or friends of the ruler, and so we must be wary of bias here. People are often willing to talk about the qualities of their famous relatives, but less willing to divulge damaging information. This ancient historian has provided valuable information for hundreds of other historians throughout the centuries, and his account of Cleisthenes' actions forms a major part of the information we have about Cleisthenes of Athens.

In 1890, a papyrus was discovered in Egypt that contained an almost complete copy of a work called the "Athenian Constitution." In the late fourth century BC, the philosopher Aristotle and his pupils wrote 158 "constitutions" of Greek city-states as part of their collection of evidence for the study of political science. The portion that has survived for so many years is about eighty pages long and it is in two sections. The first section provides a constitutional history of Athens up to 404 BC.

Aristotle is considered by many to be one of the greatest minds of classical Greece. He was a scientist, a mathematician, and a philosopher. He was the pupil of the famous philosopher Plato in Athens, and later went on to be the tutor of a more famous pupil, Alexander the Great. The "Athenian Constitution" was probably written by one of Aristotle's pupils, but as this writer's name has not come down to us through history, the work is published under Aristotle's name. The pupil who composed this document relied on Herodotus for much of his information about how Cleisthenes came to power in Athens, but he obviously had other sources of information as well. Aristotle's *Politics*, a textbook of political science, provides general information about how the Greeks governed themselves and discusses which type of constitutions are best and how they can be successful. This book mentions Cleisthenes only twice by name but discusses the democracy that he began to develop in Athens.

Archaeology acts as a support for literary sources. Archaeologists discover and analyze essential clues that often fit together with the statements from ancient writings like the pieces of a jigsaw puzzle. For the story of Cleisthenes, we are indebted to hundreds of archaeologists who have discovered thousands of artifacts and ancient sites. A fragment of pottery with a name written on it, or the ruins of an ancient building, can lend support to what the ancient writers have claimed.

The written works we do have in our possession have reached us because of the tradition of copying manuscripts. The ancient texts that survive are frequently copies of earlier copies. They are written on papyrus or on vellum or parchment (made from animal skins). Some have been discovered by archaeologists. Others have survived in monasteries, where monks and nuns during the Middle Ages preserved them.

The only way to duplicate copies in ancient times was to copy by hand, using a stylus, or reed pen, and ink. There were no facilities for printing or producing mass copies. There were no photocopiers, computers, or printing presses. The person copying the work may not have understood the text being copied. The original may have been damaged or smudged and hard to read, making the whole business of copying it accurately very difficult. It is an enormous credit to hundreds of clever and devoted scholars and teachers that we have as much information as we do.

GLOSSARY

acropolis An area of high ground with fortifications. The literal meaning is "high city." A place to which the population of a city could retreat and find protection in times of danger. Often used as a religious place, with temples in honor of the deities of the city.

agora An open area in the middle of a Greek city used for markets and as a meeting place. Often, public buildings were constructed around the agora.

Alcmaeonidae The family Cleisthenes was born into. An important aristocratic family in Athens.

archon A magistrate in Athens who served a one-year term.

Areopagus A council of men who had all been archons, named after the hill where the council met.

aristocrat A member of an important, rich, land-owning family.

Aristotle A philosopher who studied in Athens and later, after tutoring

Alexander the Great, returned to set up a school called the Lyceum. He lived from 384 to 322 BC.

Athene A Greek goddess, the daughter of Zeus and Metis. Athene was the goddess of wisdom and war, and the patron goddess of Athens.

Attica The countryside surrounding Athens.

citizen A free man of Athens who had privileges and duties in the government of his city-state.

council or assembly. A governing body like the Council of Five Hundred in Athens.

demarch The magistrate of a deme.

deme A local, territorial district in Attica, like a village or neighborhood.

democracy "Rule by the people." A political system in which all citizens have their say in government.

Herodotus A historian who lived from around 484 to 420 BC. Herodotus wrote a history of the Greek people and is sometimes referred to as the "father of history."

hoplite A heavily armed soldier.

isonomia A system of government in which all citizens are equal under the law ("iso" means equal, "nomia" means law). Cleisthenes' constitution was described as isonomia.

krater A large vessel, like a vase, in which water and wine were mixed together.

ostracism Banishment or exile. Athenians, after Cleisthenes, could take a vote to exile an unpopular person from Athens for ten years. Citizens wrote or scratched the name of the leader on ostraka, or shards of pottery.

polis An independent city-state, consisting of the city and the countryside around it.

prytany A group of fifty men, chosen by lot from one tribe, that governed for one-tenth of the year in Athens.

tyrant A Greek ruler who gained power unconstitutionally and then ruled with absolute power.

FOR MORE INFORMATION

American Classical League
Miami University
Oxford, OH 45056
e-mail: info@aclclassics.org
Web site: http://www.aclclassics.org

The Classical Association
Room 323, Third Floor
Senate House
London WC1E 7HU
England
+44 020-7862-8706
e-mail: Clare.Roberts@sas.ac.uk
Web site: http://www.sas.ac.uk/icls/
    classass

International Plutarch Society
Department of History
Utah State University
0710 Old Main Hill
Logan, UT 84322-0710
Web site: http://www.usu.edu/
    history/plout.htm

National Junior Classical League
Miami University
Oxford, OH 45056-1694
(513) 529-7741
Web site: http://www.njcl.org

WEB SITES
Due to the changing nature of Internet links, the Rosen Publishing Group, Inc., has developed an online list of Web sites related to the subject of this book. This site is updated regularly. Please use this link to access the list:

http://www.rosenlinks.com/lag/clei/

For Further Reading

Burrell, Roy. *The Greeks*. Oxford, England: Oxford University Press, 1989.

Connolly, Peter. *Ancient Greece*. Oxford, England: Oxford University Press, 2001.

Hull, Robert. *Greece*. London: Wayland, 1997.

Macdonald, Fiona. *The Ancient Greece*. New York: Kingfisher, 2002.

Macdonald, Fiona. *How Would You Survive as an Ancient Greek?* London: Watts, 1995.

Peach, Susan. *The Greeks*. London: Usborne, 1990.

Pearson, Anne. *Ancient Greece*. London: Dorling Kindersley, 1992.

Pearson, Anne. *What Do We Know About the Ancient Greeks?* London: Simon and Schuster, 1992.

Bibliography

Aristotle. *The Athenian Constitution.*
London: Penguin, 1984.

Aristotle. *Politics.* London: Penguin, 1962.

Boardman, John, ed. *Oxford History of
the Classical World.* Oxford, England:
Oxford University Press, 1986.

Burrell, Roy. *The Greeks.* Oxford, England:
Oxford University Press, 1989.

Demoen, Kristoffel, ed. *The Greek City
from Antiquity to Present.* Louvain,
Belgium: Peeters, 2001.

Ehrenberg, Victor. *From Solon to
Socrates.* London: Methuen, 1983.

Grant, Michael. *Greek and Roman
Historians.* London: Routledge, 1995.

Hart, John. *Herodotus and Greek History.*
London: Self Publishing, 1993.

Herodotus. *The Histories.* London:
Penguin, 1954.

Hornblower, Simon, ed. *Oxford
Companion to Classical Civilisation.*
Oxford, England: Oxford University
Press, 1998.

McGlew, James F. *Citizens on Stage: Comedy and Political Culture in the Athenian Democracy.* Ann Arbor, MI: University of Michigan Press, 2002.

Murray, Oswyn. *Early Greece.* London: Fontana, 1993.

Sekunda, Nick. *The Ancient Greeks.* London: Osprey, 1986.

INDEX

A

ABOUT THE AUTHOR

Sarah Parton was born in West Yorkshire, England, in 1966. She went to school in Bradford, and then studied classics at Cambridge University. She gained an MA in publishing from Loughborough University, and now lives and works at a boarding school in Leicestershire. She is married with two sons.

CREDITS

EDITOR

Jake Goldberg

DESIGN

Evelyn Horovicz